STARS AND STRIPES

The white stars, set against a field of blue in the original design Congress suggested for the American flag, were intended to represent a new constellation. The stripes were to depict a unification of forces for a common cause. Both symbols are often lifted from the flag to use alone in a design, and even then, their symbolism is still evident. They clearly summon patriotic feelings.

I hope you enjoy blending these two very powerful symbols into your own quilts, banners, and wall hangings. They will lend a wonderful patriotic flair to any room decorated in an Americana theme.

Nancy Southerland-Holmes

General Directions

1. Before you begin a project, read through the directions and list of materials. Gather necessary supplies and fabrics.
2. Examine the photos and drawings to help you understand the quilt assembly.
3. When required, full-size templates are included on a pullout pattern insert in the center of this booklet. For simple squares and rectangles, cutting dimensions, including ¼"-wide seam allowances, are given instead of templates. If you plan to make several versions of one design, you may wish to draw and cut templates from stiff paper or lightweight cardboard for squares or rectangles needed. Or, rotary cut these simple shapes.
4. Trace patterns printed on the pages of the booklet onto tissue paper to avoid destroying patterns or directions on the reverse side. Include all lines, markings, and labels for cutting reference.
5. If you have never pieced or quilted by hand, I encourage you to try a small project. As a child, I learned these hand arts from my mother. For me, the process of drawing needle and thread through fabric brings joy to quiltmaking, not the speed with which a quilt can be finished with machine methods. While I favor piecing quilts by hand, I do appreciate the speed and precision of a sewing machine. Use the method you prefer.
6. Be creative. Use some or all of the designs in this booklet to create an Americana sampler. Or, make enough blocks to create a bed-size quilt instead of a small wall hanging. Consider using the appliqué motifs on sweatshirts, jean jackets, children's pockets, worn dungaree knees, and babies' bibs.

TOOLS AND SUPPLIES

You will need some basic equipment to make these designs: sharp scissors; erasable fabric marking pen; straight pins; short, fine quilting needles; your favorite thimble; a ruler; a smooth, flat tracing and cutting surface; and a pleasant, well-lit place to sit and enjoy the stitching! Rotary-cutting tools are also an option.

Use your favorite water-soluble marking pen, pencil, or chalk to draw quilting guidelines onto the completed quilt top. Always test for removability on fabric scraps before marking an entire quilt top.

Choose a neutral-colored thread for piecing, whether by hand or machine. Beige, gray, and off-white are good choices. Match thread color to appliqué, not to the background.

Hand quilting thread is coarser than regular sewing thread and coated to reduce tangling as you sew. Choose white thread to show off fine quilting stitches. Red or blue quilting thread may be used if white is too bold against colored backgrounds or if you prefer inconspicuous quilting stitches.

Keep a supply of sewing machine needles on hand for machine piecing. For hand piecing and quilting, use sizes 9, 10, or 12 Betweens. For appliqué, a size 10 Sharp works well. Needles do bend, break, and drop out of sight. Determine your favorite needle size for handwork and invest in a good supply.

AMERICANA COLORS

For years, I have enjoyed making Americana items to use in our home year-round as well as for special holiday decorating. I love Americana colors and motifs—antique prints with tiny stars, rich, blue, homespun plaids, and red-and-white stripes of all widths.

There is always room in my fabric collection for a deep, rich red. It's the color of the little prairie schoolhouse, country hearts, juicy strawberries, checkered tablecloths, holly berries, crisp apples, and my children's rosy cheeks after playtime.

American "true blues," from deep navy to colonial shades, show up in painted country furniture, enameled spatterware, children's overalls, and the striped ticking on antique feather beds. "The blue cup" in my kitchen is an old enameled tin piece that holds loose change for ice cream cones, bubble gum, or cold lemonade on a hot summer day—the simple pleasures of an all-American childhood.

White balances vibrant reds and blues in patriotic themes. I love vintage cotton muslin, old flour sacks, and handmade lace borders hemstitched to tablecloths, dresser scarves, and bed linens. White evokes visions of picket fences, hillsides blanketed with daisies, glossy white porch chairs, and christening gowns. Pure, white soap reminds me of my favorite aunt who was born in 1900 and made her own soap until a few years before she passed on, declaring it was "better than bought soap." She always admired my quilting stitches. I always admired her complexion.

The vibrant colors I've used in these beguiling little quilts reflect my personal color preferences. You may prefer lighter or darker, brighter or duller shades. Use colors you like and that will enhance your decor.

FABRIC SELECTION

I recommend 100% cotton fabrics for your quilts and their backings for the easiest stitching and best results. Wool flannel is another wonderful alternative for these small projects. Preshrink cotton fabrics and thoroughly steam press woolens before cutting.

Work from your scrap bag whenever possible, particularly when ⅛-yard or smaller pieces are required. Fat quarters (quarter-yard pieces cut 18" x 22") are available at quilt shops and are often just the right size for smaller pattern pieces. When yardages are given, you can expect to have scraps to use in future quilting projects.

Some of the projects have a timeworn appearance, accomplished by staining the fabrics with a concentrated tea or coffee solution. (My choice depends on which I have in my kitchen at the time!)

Fabric can be stained before cutting and sewing, or after a quilt top is pieced. When deciding if a fabric or quilt would be enhanced by "aging" it, I imagine if, once stained, it would remind me of a handmade treasure pulled from an old family trunk. Simple prints and plain designs are the best candidates. Muslin also stains well.

To "age" fabrics by staining:
1. Make a large pot of tea or coffee and pour into a container large enough to completely immerse your fabric or quilt top.

2. Immerse and stir until fabric is completely saturated with the dark solution. Soak until liquid cools.
3. Wring out fabric and dry on hot setting in dryer to set stain. For deeper "aging," blot randomly with a second staining and dry again. Press as needed.

BATTING AND BACKING

I prefer cotton batting because it gives these quilts the look and feel our foremothers achieved when making the first American quilts. It is thin and compact and easier to quilt with tiny hand stitches. Closely spaced quilting is required to prevent cotton batting from shifting and separating.

Choose a backing fabric with a smooth, plain weave for easy quilting. Muslin shows off quilting stitches beautifully but prints are nice, too. (They can hide less-than-perfect quilting stitches.)

BASIC TECHNIQUES

Piecing

Piece by hand or machine, depending on your preference and skill. You can combine both methods in one project—hand piece the blocks, then machine stitch the sashing and borders to the blocks to assemble the quilt top.

To piece by hand or machine:
1. Use a neutral-colored thread.
2. Stitch exact ¼"-wide seams. It may be helpful to mark the seam lines on the wrong side of each piece before stitching.
3. Take 10 to 12 stitches per inch.
4. Sew the smallest pieces of a block together first, forming units to join together until the block is complete.

Note: When several points or angles come together, as in many star patterns, begin and end stitching at the point where seam lines intersect instead of beginning and ending at the raw edges at each end of the seam.

5. When piecing is completed, press seams open or to one side to flatten them for easier quilting.

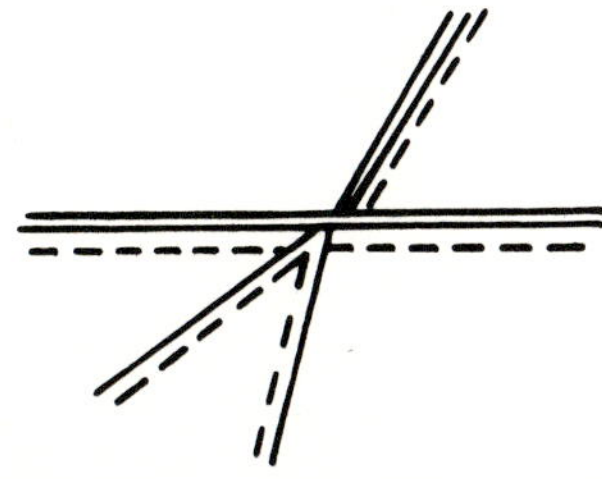

6. For hand piecing, thread a quilting needle with an 18"-long, single strand of thread and knot one end. With right sides together and seam lines matching, stitch the pieces together with a simple running stitch. Begin and end stitching at seam intersections, not at outer edge of patches. End with a backstitch,

pulling the needle through the loop as you tighten the thread against the last stitch.

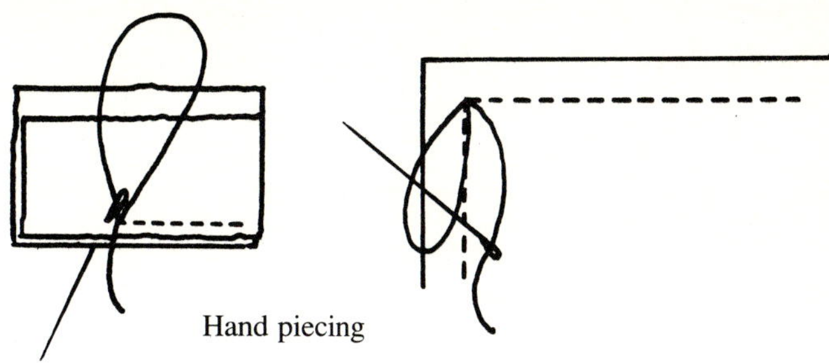

Hand piecing

Hand Appliqué

Traditional needle-turned appliqué lends a classic look to a quilt. Appliqué templates include a ⅛"-wide turn-under allowance.

To appliqué:
1. Cut appliqués using template provided. Pin or baste in position on background fabric.
2. Thread a size 11 Sharp needle with an 18"-long, single strand of thread that matches appliqué. Knot one end.
3. Using the point of the needle, turn under raw edges of appliqué and hold in place with finger while drawing thread from beneath appliqué through to the top. Knot should be under appliqué.
4. Stitch in place with a tiny, blind-hemming stitch through folded edge of appliqué and background fabric. Space stitches ¹⁄₁₆" to ⅛" apart. Space them closer together on sharp curves and points.

5. When stitching is complete, knot thread close to appliqué and bury between appliqué and background fabric.

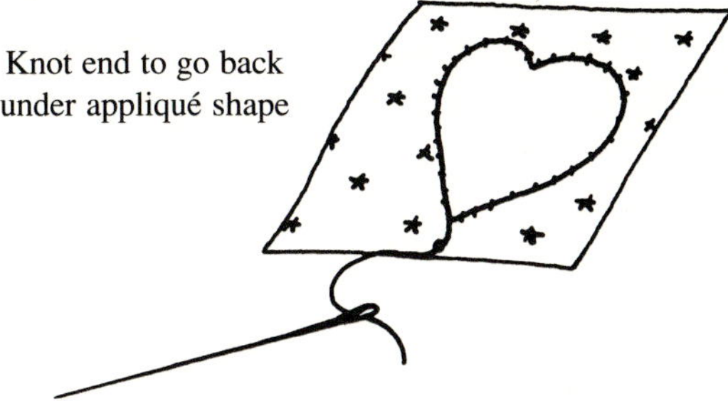

Note: When one appliqué piece overlaps another, the edge of the lower piece is left unturned (raw) to eliminate a ridge that would show through the completed work.

Preparing for Quilting
1. Cut batting and prepare backing, making each 2" larger all around than completed quilt top.

2. Spread and smooth backing fabric, face down, on a large, flat surface. Use masking tape to secure edges.

3. Smooth batting over backing. Place quilt top on batting and smooth in place.

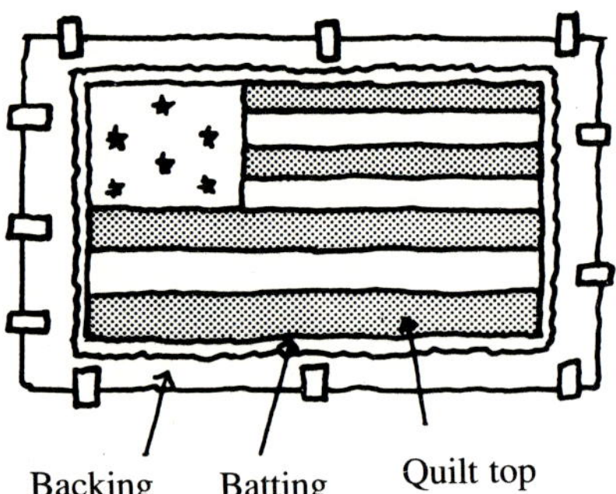

Backing   Batting   Quilt top

4. Pin and baste the layers together, using a long needle and white or a light-colored thread. Begin at center and baste with long stitches in a large X, extending to the corners. Fill in with parallel rows, spaced 8" to 10" apart. Baste around outer edge. Quilt design is not shown in illustration.

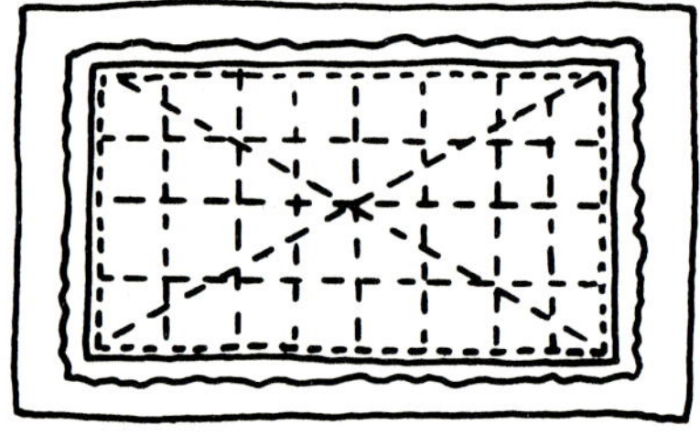

Hand Quilting

Hand quilting is a series of simple running stitches, which follow a pattern and go through all three quilt layers to hold them together. It can frame and highlight block pieces, outline appliqués, and create movement and texture in the quilt's surface. Decorative quilting designs are used to highlight and fill in large, open areas. Quilting can outline elaborate motifs or can be as simple as straight lines sewn in crisscross fashion across the entire quilt surface.

To hand quilt:

1. Thread a quilting needle (the smaller, the better) with a single strand of quilting thread and knot the end.

2. Insert needle through quilt top and batting at a seam line and tug gently until knot "pops" through the top and catches in batting.

3. Take tiny stitches, striving for 8 to 10 stitches per inch. Don't worry if stitches aren't perfect. They will add primitive appeal to the finished piece.

Note: Quilting suggestions are given with each project.

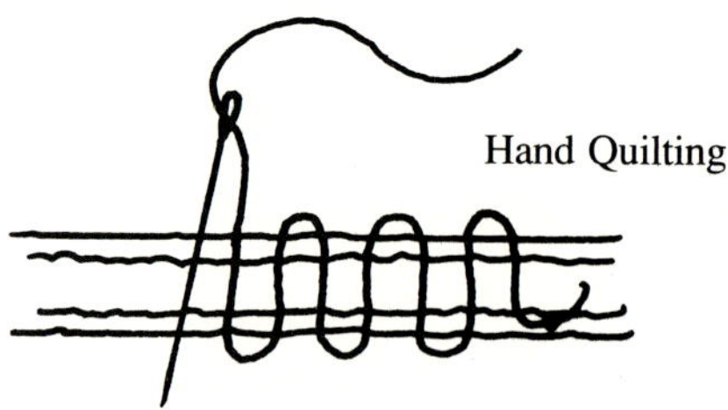

Hand Quilting

4. When you run out of thread, make a small knot close to quilt top. Insert needle and pull knot back through quilt layers. Bring needle up through quilt top and snip thread at the surface. Remove basting except around outer edges. Bind raw edges. See below for binding techniques.

Tie Quilting

Instead of quilting stitches, you can tie the quilt layers together. It is often used on pieced quilts made of heavier fabrics, such as wool. Tying is easier and faster than hand quilting and is a good way to introduce children to quilting.

To tie a quilt:

1. Layer and baste quilt as shown at left.

2. Thread a 3"-long needle with a 30" strand of cotton crochet thread or perle cotton. Take a single stitch through the layers and cut thread, leaving 3"-long ends. Tie in a square knot next to the quilt surface.

3. Continue across quilt top, placing ties at block corners or in continuous rows. Space them no more than 5" to 6" apart. Ties can be placed to create a decorative motif, such as a star or heart.

Tie Quilting

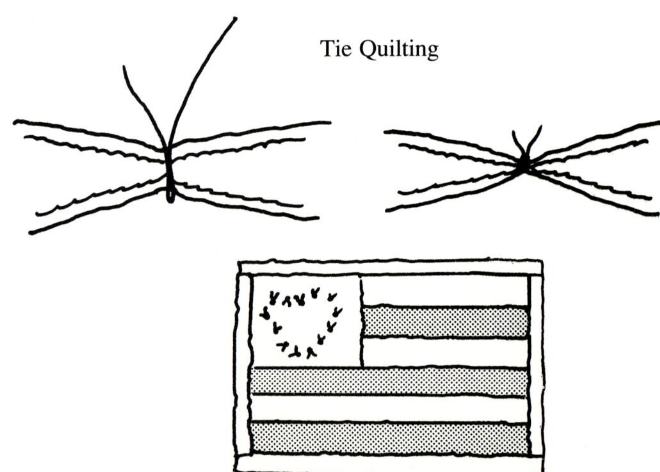

Binding the Quilt

Binding finishes the raw edges and "frames" the quilt. Choose a rolled binding (cut in one with the backing) or one cut from strips and attached to the edges.

For rolled binding:

1. Cut backing fabric 2" larger all around than finished quilt top. Layer with batting and top and quilt or tie as desired.

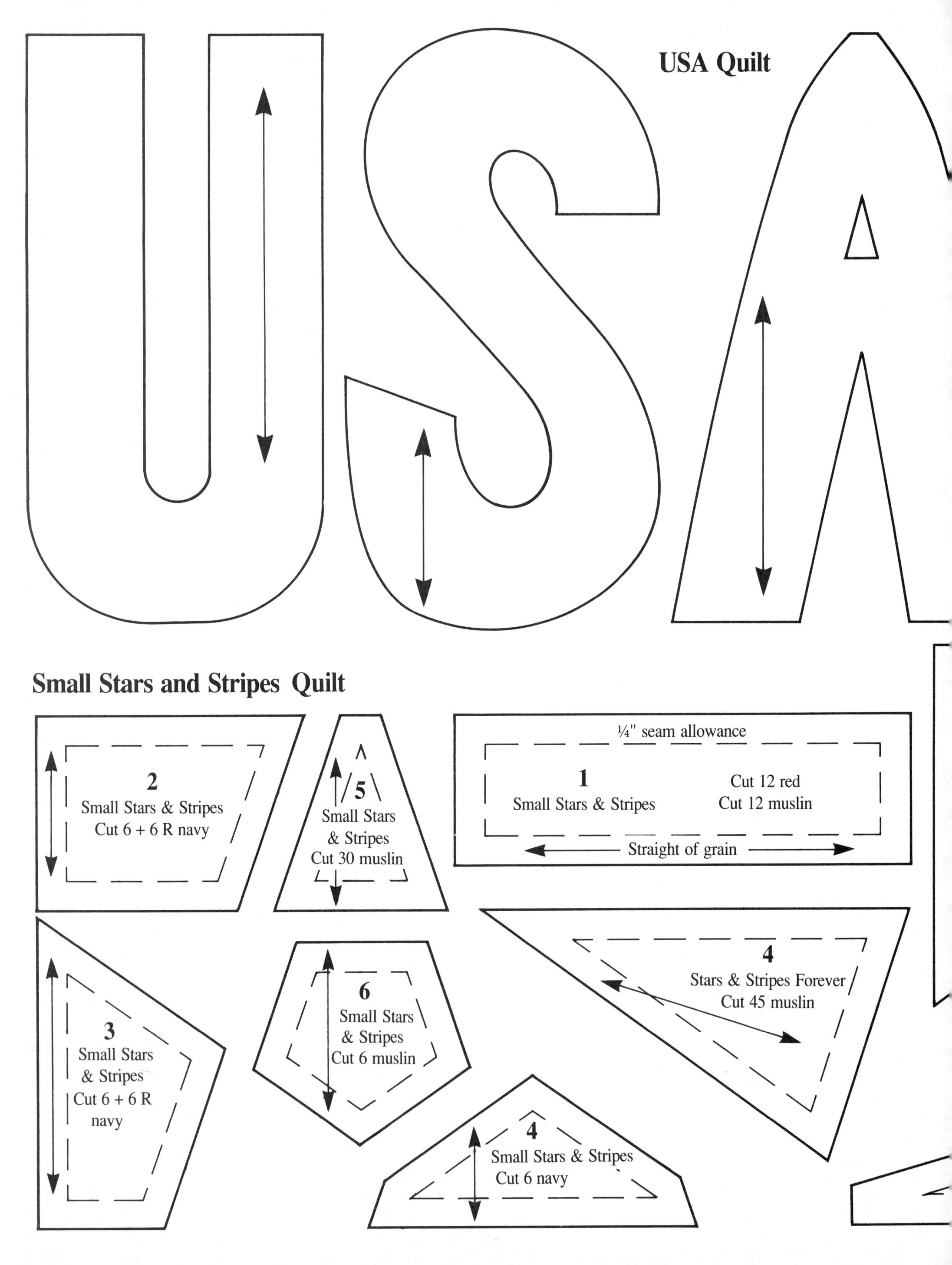

USA Quilt

Small Stars and Stripes Quilt

2
Small Stars & Stripes
Cut 6 + 6 R navy

5
Small Stars
& Stripes
Cut 30 muslin

¼" seam allowance

1
Small Stars & Stripes

Cut 12 red
Cut 12 muslin

Straight of grain

3
Small Stars
& Stripes
Cut 6 + 6 R
navy

6
Small Stars
& Stripes
Cut 6 muslin

4
Stars & Stripes Forever
Cut 45 muslin

4
Small Stars & Stripes
Cut 6 navy

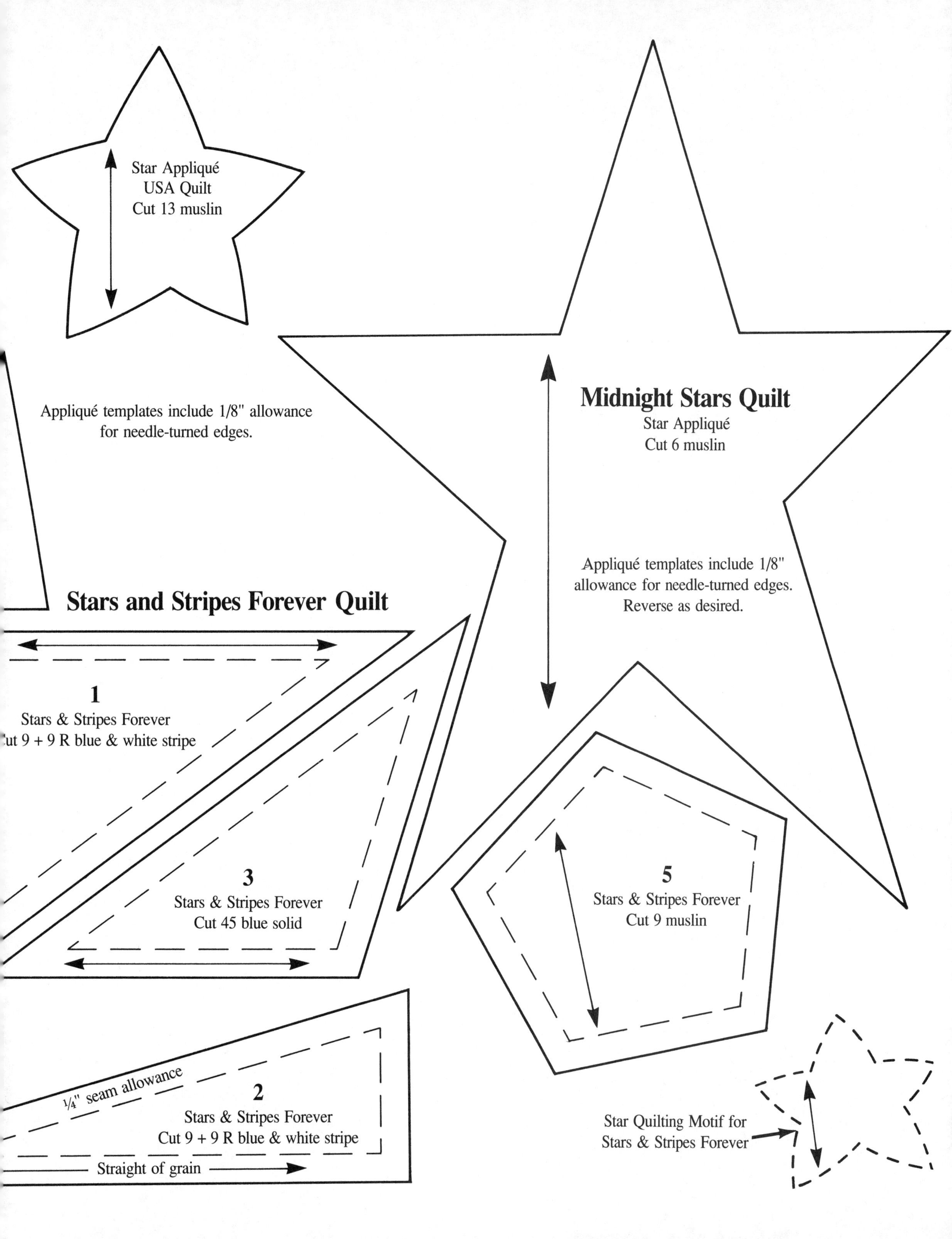

Star Appliqué
USA Quilt
Cut 13 muslin

Appliqué templates include 1/8" allowance
for needle-turned edges.

Midnight Stars Quilt
Star Appliqué
Cut 6 muslin

Appliqué templates include 1/8"
allowance for needle-turned edges.
Reverse as desired.

Stars and Stripes Forever Quilt

1
Stars & Stripes Forever
Cut 9 + 9 R blue & white stripe

3
Stars & Stripes Forever
Cut 45 blue solid

5
Stars & Stripes Forever
Cut 9 muslin

1/4" seam allowance

2
Stars & Stripes Forever
Cut 9 + 9 R blue & white stripe

Straight of grain

Star Quilting Motif for
Stars & Stripes Forever

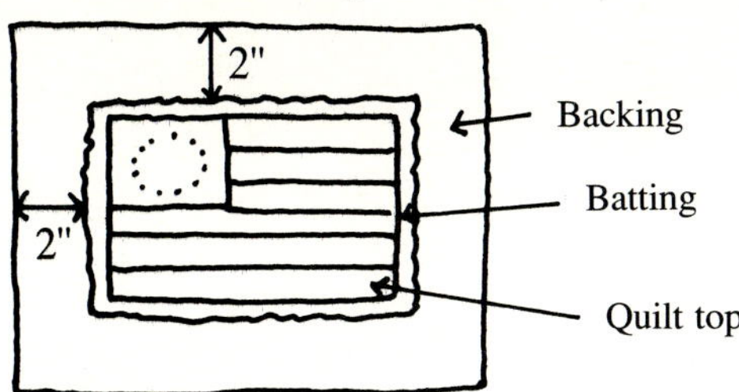

2. Trim batting even with quilt top and trim backing so it extends ¾" beyond quilt top edges.
3. Double and roll extra backing around the quilt raw edges and slipstitch in place. Do sides first, then top and bottom edges.

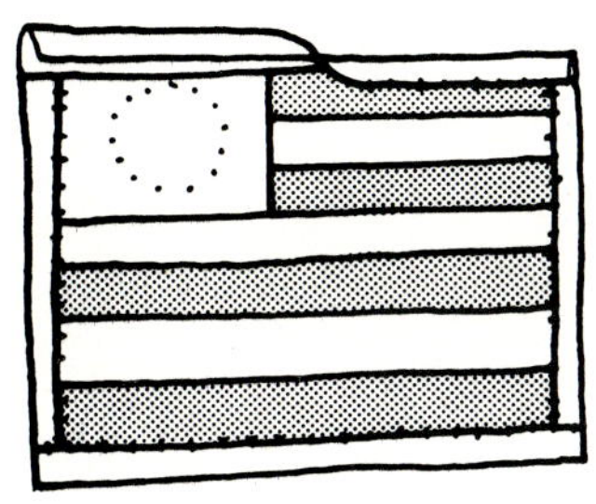

For separate bias binding:
1. Cut enough 1"-wide bias from binding fabric to seam together into a continuous strip to fit the finished quilt. Allow an extra 2" for overlapping and turning ends where they meet.
2. With right sides together, stitch the binding to the quilt by hand or machine, using a ¼"-wide seam and mitering corners.

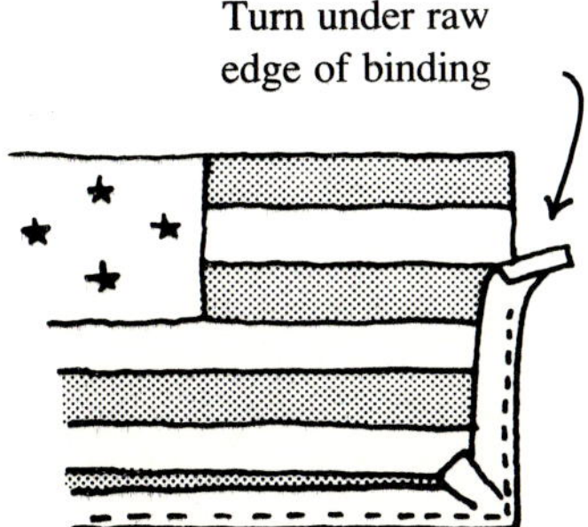

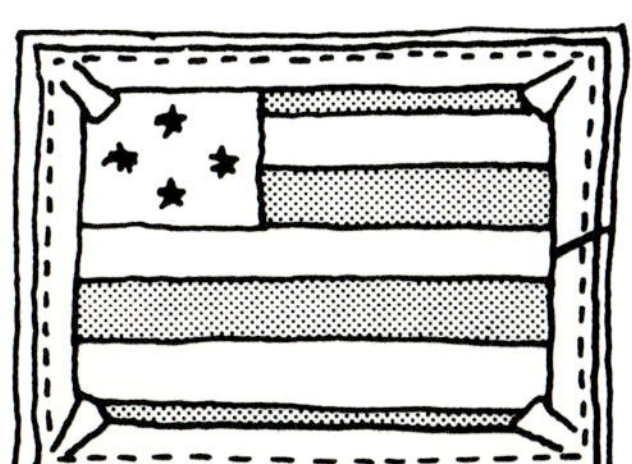

3. Fold binding over quilt edge, turning under the raw edge; slipstitch in place along seam line and at corners.

Quilt binding can also be cut on straight of grain. When attached, it resembles a rolled binding.

For separate straight-grain binding:
1. Cut 1"-wide strips for each edge of quilt, making them each 2" longer than actual edge measurement.
2. With right sides together and raw edges even, stitch a binding strip to each short edge of quilt. Fold over raw edges as shown for bias binding and slipstitch in place on back side of quilt.

3. Add two remaining binding strips in same manner, turning in and stitching raw edges at ends.

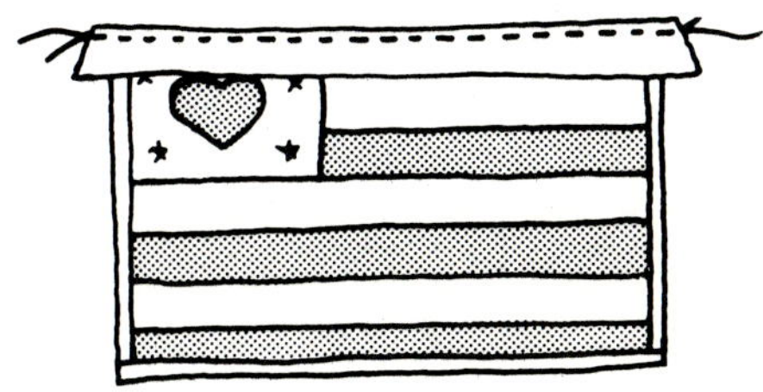

USA Quilt

Finished Size: 22¾" x 24¼"

This was the first quilt I stitched when my ideas for this collection of patriotic designs began to materialize. It combines traditional piecing with appliqué, tie quilting, and hand quilting—all in one project. It is still one of my favorites. To make it, I really "worked" my scrap bag to find the right remnants for this true Americana, "make-do" quilt.

Materials: 44"-wide fabric
¼ yd. muslin for stars and white stripes
½ yd. navy blue pindot for top and bottom borders and star background
½ yd. red cotton for letters, borders, and red stripes
⅛ yd. navy blue cotton for flagpole
⅛ yd. bold red-and-white stripe
1½ yds. white-on-white pindot print for background, borders, backing, and binding
Crochet thread to tie-quilt the "stars"
Batting and thread to finish

Cutting

Using the patterns provided on the pattern pullout insert, cut 13 star appliqués from muslin. From the red fabric, cut the appliqué letters USA.

Note: Appliqué patterns include a ⅛" turn-under allowance. Set appliqués aside as you cut and assemble the flag quilt top.

☆ From navy blue pindot, cut 1 piece, 5½" x 6¾", for the upper left corner of flag. Cut 2 strips, each 3¼" x 22¾", for outer top and bottom borders.

☆ From red-and-white stripe, cut 1 strip, 1 " x 9¼", for first stripe (with stripes perpendicular to the long side of the strip). Cut 1 strip, 1½" x 4", for part of the seventh stripe (with stripes parallel to the long side of the strip).

☆ From muslin, cut 1 strip, 1 " x 9¼", for second stripe; 1 strip, 2" x 9¼", for fourth stripe; 1 strip, 1 " x 15½" for sixth stripe; and 1 strip, 1½" x 15½", for eighth stripe.

☆ From the red cotton, cut 1 strip, 1½" x 9¼", for third stripe; 1 strip, 1 " x 15½", for fifth stripe; 1 strip, 1½" x 12", for part of seventh stripe; and 1 strip, 1¼" x 15½", for ninth stripe. For outer side borders, cut 2 strips, each 1½" x 18¾".

☆ From navy blue cotton, cut 1 piece, ¾" x 18¾", for flagpole.

☆ From white-on-white pindot, cut 1 strip, 2" x 15½", for top of pieced flag. For appliquéd piece under flag, cut 1 piece, 7" x 15½". For inner side border (left), cut 1 strip, 2¾" x 18¾". For inner side border (right), cut 1 strip, 3¼" x 18¾".

Directions

1. Position and appliqué 6 stars to the top blue border and 7 to the bottom blue border. See appliqué how-tos (page 3). The primitive style of this quilt is enhanced by rotating the stars slightly as you position them so the points thrust out in different directions. As you appliqué, try to keep the points and inner corners of the stars from being too exact. For a more primitive look, it's OK if they are a little rounded.

2. Position and appliqué the USA letters in the lower right-hand corner of the large white strip as shown in the diagram below.

3. Piece the flag section of the quilt, following the piecing diagram below. Press seams to one side (toward the darker fabric when possible).

4. Next, add the white panels to the top and bottom of the flag. Then, piece the vertical strips shown to the right (1 white, 1 red) and left (1 blue, 1 white, and 1 red) of the flag. Press seams to one side. Stitch pieced strips to the flag.

Finally, add the star borders to the top and bottom edges.

5. Layer the completed quilt top with the batting and backing. Baste the layers together and hand quilt (page 4). Quilting stitches on the quilt shown are spaced ¼" in from the edge around each piece of the quilt top and around each star's edge. Stars are quilted ⅛" in from the appliquéd edge. USA letters are outline quilted and also ⅛" in from appliquéd edge.

6. Using lengths of crochet thread, tie-quilt 50 evenly spaced "stars" through the blue background of the flag. See tie-quilting (page 4). Five rows of 10 knots might seem a bit tedious, but the results are worth it!

7. Bind the raw edges (page 4).

Midnight Stars Quilt

Finished Size: 17⅛" x 32¾"

This simple six-block quilt, with its large, friendly five-point stars appliquéd on a light blue ground, is an easy beginner's quilt.

> **Materials:** 44"-wide fabric
> 1¼ yds. muslin for stars and backing
> ½ yd. blue-and-white gingham (tiny checks)
> ⅛ yd. red-and-white striped fabric for sashing squares
> ½ yd. navy blue solid for sashing and borders
> ¼ yd. red solid for binding
> Batting and thread to finish

Cutting

Using the template provided on the pattern pullout insert, cut 6 stars from the muslin.

☆ From the gingham, cut 6 rectangles, each 6¼" x 8".

☆ From the red-and-white stripe, cut 6 sashing squares, each 1⅞" square.

☆ From the navy blue, cut 3 center vertical sashing pieces, each 2⅞" x 8". Cut 4 horizontal sashing pieces, each 2⅞" x 6¼". Cut 2 side borders, each 1⅞" x 28½". For the top and bottom borders, cut 2 pieces, each 1⅞" x 13½".

Directions

1. Center and hand appliqué a star on each gingham rectangle. Remember, no two stars in the universe are exactly alike, so reverse a few so the points are not all uniform in each block. It's OK if the points are not "pointy." It gives a more homespun look.

2. Set blocks together with sashing and sashing squares. Add side borders. Sew corner blocks to ends of top and bottom border strips and stitch to the quilt.

3. Layer the completed quilt top with batting and backing and baste layers together (page 4).

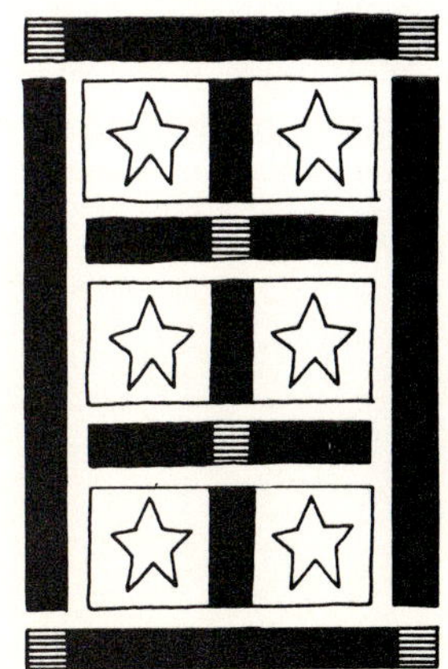

4. Hand quilt, stitching around each piece ¼" in from the seam line and ¼" in from appliquéd edge around each star.

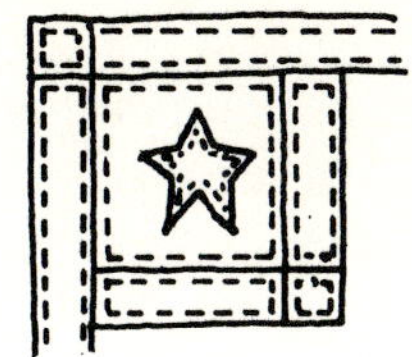

5. Bind the raw edges (page 4).

Small Stars and Stripes Quilt

Finished Size: 11¾" x 14"

This little quilt was inspired by Early American antique doll quilts, made when learning needlework was a vital part of a young girl's education. I'm sure bold combinations of red, white, and blue were as pleasing to children then as now.

> **Materials:** 44"-wide fabric
> ⅛ yd. red solid for stripes and binding
> ⅛ yd. navy blue solid for star background
> ¼ yd. muslin for stars and stripes
> ⅛ yd. blue-and-white striped fabric for borders
> ½ yd. backing
> Batting and thread to finish

Cutting

Use templates found on the pattern pullout insert.

☆ From the red, cut 12 of Template 1.

☆ From the navy, cut 6 and 6 reversed each of Templates 2 and 3. Cut 6 of Template 4.

☆ From the muslin, cut 12 of Template 1; cut 30 of Template 5; cut 6 of Template 6.

☆ From the striped fabric, cut 2 pieces, each 1¼" x 12", for side borders and 2 pieces, each 1¼" x 11½", for top and bottom borders.

Directions

1. Piece 6 striped blocks in red-white-red-white sequence. Piece 6 star blocks, following the piecing diagram.

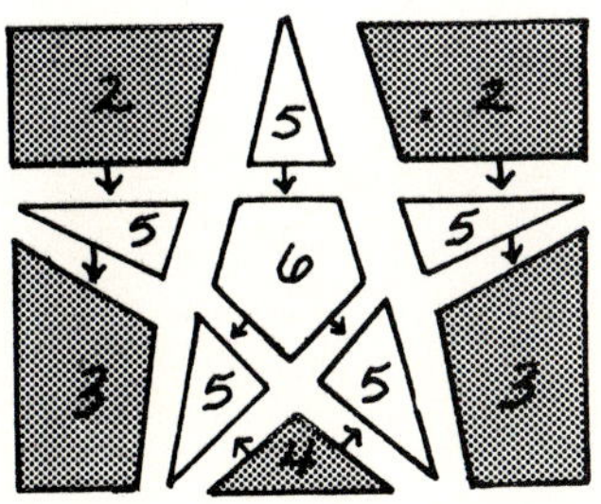

2. Assemble blocks into quilt top, referring to the photo on the front cover for placement.
3. Add side borders to quilt top, then top and bottom borders.
4. Layer completed quilt top with batting and backing and baste layers together (page 4).
5. Quilt ⅛" inside the seam lines around each piece, matching thread color to each piece.
6. Bind edges with red binding cut on the straight grain (page 5).

Stars and Stripes Forever Quilt

Finished Size: 26½" x 26½"

A new red-and-white star print and vintage blue-and-white cotton ticking frame the pentagons surrounding these five-point, pieced stars. Piece additional blocks of this design to make a fabulous bed-size quilt, perfect for a bedroom gone patriotic! An all-American baby would be blessed to have such a heritage keepsake, made in the nine-block version shown.

Materials: 44"-wide fabric
½ yd. muslin for stars and sashing squares
½ yd. red star print for sashing
½ yd. blue solid for pentagons and borders
½ yd. blue-and-white ticking for star background and bias binding
1 yd. backing
Batting and thread to finish

Cutting

Use templates found on the pattern pullout insert.
☆ From the muslin, cut 45 of Template 4. Cut 9 of Template 5. Cut 8 pieces, each 2" x 2", for the sashing squares.
☆ From the red star print, cut 12 sashing strips, each 2" x 6½". Cut 4 sashing strips, each 2" x 21½".
☆ From the blue solid, cut 45 of Template 3. Cut 2 pieces, each 1½" x 24 ½", for the side borders and 2 pieces, each 1½" x 26½", for the top and bottom borders.
☆ From the blue-and-white ticking, cut 9 and 9 reversed each of Templates 1 and 2.

Directions

1. Piece 9 star blocks, following the piecing diagram below.

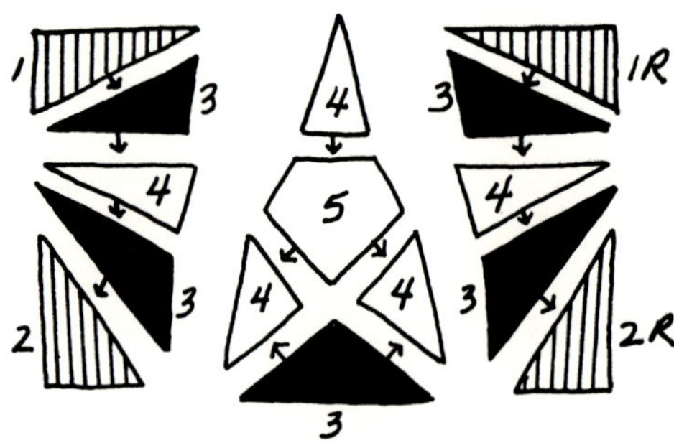

2. Assemble 3 rows of star blocks joined with short sashing strips.
3. Assemble 2 rows of short sashing strips connected with white blocks as shown.
4. Join rows of blocks with sashing strips and add side sashing.
5. Sew a muslin sashing square to the short ends of the top and bottom sashing strips. Attach to top and bottom edges to complete the quilt top.

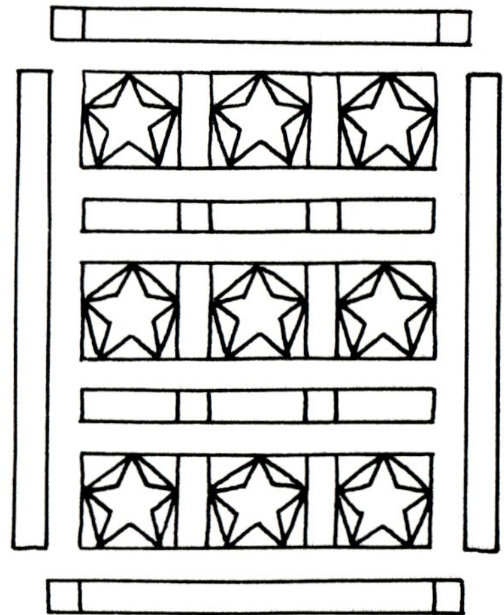

Add the blue side borders, then the top and bottom borders.
6. Layer the quilt top with batting and backing and baste the layers together as shown on page 4.
7. Hand quilt ⅛" in from edges of all stars, sashings, and borders. Quilt the star motif (available on the pattern pullout) on the corner muslin sashing blocks. Quilting thread to match the red and blue fabrics was used in the quilting. To highlight fine hand-quilting stitches, use white quilting thread throughout.
8. Bind the raw edges (page 4).